AF578450

JACQUELINE GORDON CAIN
Beautiful Faith
Learn To Lean On God

Beautiful Faith

By: Jacqueline Gordon Cain

Hebrews 11:1-2 (NKJV)
"[1]Now faith is the substance of things hoped for, the evidence of things not seen. [2]For by it the elders obtained a good testimony"

2022 by Jacqueline Cain Ministries, Norcross, GA
Printed in the United States of America

-
Scriptures quotations marked N.I.V. (The New International Version), A.M.P, K.J.V.. N,K.J.V (New King James Version), N.S.B.A (American Standard Bible)
copyright 1980,1982, by Thomas Nelson, Inc. Publisher

Beautiful Faith

Jacqueline Gordon Cain

ISBN 9798811579358

Learn to grow your faith by trusting in Jesus. Life can be hard, but knowing how to activate your faith, even to the size of a mustard seed, will open doors to your promises and the ability to walk in wholeness.

Table of Content

Chapter 1
What Is Faith

Hebrews 11:1 (NKJV)

"[1]Now faith is the substance of things hoped for, the evidence of things not seen. [2]For by it the elders obtained a good testimony"

This book will teach you why "Faith" is so vital and why you need to put the Lord first in your life, which equals **"Beautiful Faith."**

Beautiful Faith is simple trusting God that He will keep His word and promises.

Faith is how you please God. After all, Hebrews 11:6 states that it is impossible to please God without faith. Through faith, you accept God's promises in the Bible.

Understanding that God requires Faith, which is developed from a relationship with Him. Some of us have been taught to trust in our own intelligence and ability. As a result, we have declined to make the Lord to lead, show, or fight our battles for us.

Do you recall being a small child and knowing that your parents will always look after your needs? It was indeed "Faith," whether you understood it or not. You simply knew that you just knew that everything was fine.

Now, some of us didn't have the support of being looked after as children, but you can undoubtedly think of other ways you exercised faith. For instance, knowing that your paycheck would promptly be deposited to your account on payday.

That is why it is essential to place one's personal trust in God for both the good and bad. When we invest our faith in the proper authorities, "Jesus," we get freed of stress.

Hebrews 11:1 (NKJV)

"[1]Now faith is the substance of things hoped for, the evidence of things not seen.

"Now Faith" requires, a certain spiritual and emotional stretching, in order to believe in what is not seen but hoped for, instead of plunging under doubt, either from difficulty or uncertainty. You hold firm to hope—in other words, is assured of, takes refuge in, and rely on **"Beautiful Faith".**

Emotions were created by God for a reason. Did you realize that you can train/control your emotions? Yes, you must learn to control your emotions, especially if they force you to be placed in a bondage situation. **Good Emotions, for example (Praising God, Empathy, Love, Hope and Faithfulness). Emotions that are harmful (Negativity, Bitterness, Anger, Discontentment, Judging Spirit, Doubt).**

<u>Learning to integrate your spirit man (Spirit of God) with your emotional man (Mind & Heart)</u> can help you find a better balance in your life so that you can pursue **God's faith-filled plans**.

The spiritual requirement includes- **studying God's Word, being in right relationship with Jesus** and putting your emotions in submission to what the Lord says and not your flesh.

I have so many examples of needing faith to see my life improve, and the best way I can explain it is this: ***"I had no option but to believe - since my environment growing up and in my early years of life was highly toxic, and I was sick and tired of being sick and tired."*** So, when I'd had enough, I learned to align my spiritual man and emotions so that the Lord might build my faith from small to large.

2 Corinthians 5:7 (NIV)
"For we live by faith, not by sight."

Living by faith will increase your quality of life. Can you recall a time when you were firmly believing in something then a thought, person, or circumstance arose that caused you to doubt and abandon your faith?

The purpose of this book is to help you process your thoughts and feelings, that is why it is so important to answer questions and note your thoughts.

Make a list of times when you've questioned or abandon your faith.

James 1:2 (NIV)

"Consider it pure joy, my brothers and sisters, whenever you face trials of many kinds,"

It might be tough to keep faith in the face of adversity. It's difficult to believe in the positive when everything in your life seems to be unnecessarily difficult or just plain bad. But it is at those difficult times when faith is most crucial. In a hurricane, it can serve as a life raft. And if we are willing to look for it, faith can always be restored. Whether you're seeking for relaxing verses about patience, uplifting Bible verses about love, or consoling verses about anxiety, the Bible is an excellent location to replenish your spiritual supplies. It's called the "Good Book" for a reason: it's fantastic in getting us out of funks and into more positive mindsets.

I often tell people about how in 2013, my 23-year-old daughter died just days before I was scheduled for breast cancer surgery. You talk about having faith. I realized that if I was going to keep moving forward and not die, I'd have to summon some serious faith and trust that the Lord knew I'd be on this path long before I was born, and that God had already planned a way out for me**. "He transformed my pain into purpose." Because I have been there and done that, I am confident in my ability to teach people how to lean into faith rather than anguish.**

When we make a conscious effort to look for ways to trust God, our faith will naturally expand. When you have a need or are going through a difficult moment in your life, pray and seek the Lord's help. Then sit back and wait. Because you put your faith in Him, He will act.

Ephesians 6:10-11 & 16 (NKJV)

*[10] Finally, my brethren, be strong in the
Lord and in the power of His might. [11] Put
on the whole armor of God, that
you may be able to stand against the wiles
of the devil.*

*[16] above all, taking the shield of faith with
which you will be able to quench all the fiery
darts of the wicked one.*

Taking the shield of faith, above everything... I can deflect all of Satan's attempts to persuade me to doubt, give up, discouragement, disobedience, and sin with this shield of faith. This shield will always protect me if I believe in God and His promises and act in obedience to the faith. <u>Satan's flaming darts just glance off the shield of faith when I go forth with boldness and courage regardless of how I feel</u>

<u>or what I am tempted to do.</u> We shall face difficulties, problems, obstacles, interruptions, and delays for as long as we live on this planet. As a result, it's critical to remember how-to put-on God's "Complete" armor and trust Jesus to fight our battles while we stand on **"Beautiful Faith."**

It's critical to understand that doubt, worry, and anxiety are all enemy attacks. Taking up the shield of faith will protect us and give us the ability to defend ourselves against these attacks. Furthermore, through living in community as the body of Christ, we can assist each other in growing stronger in our faith, leading by example. **Fiery darts – Can be the past, people, relationships, sickness and loneliness**

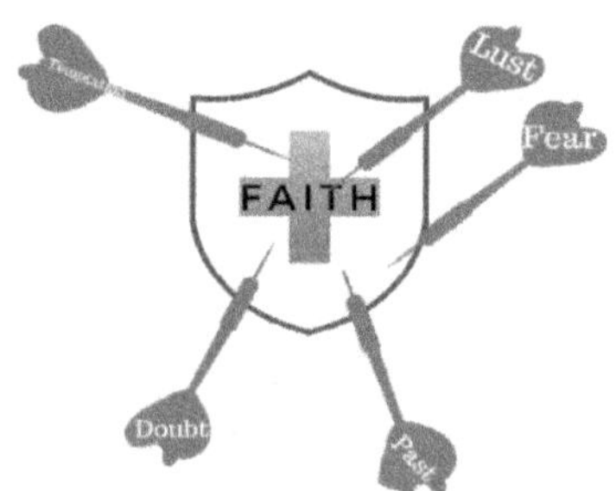

This scripture talks about …Above all — Rightly, overall, or in addition to all else. **The shield is a big, hefty shield that covers the entire body, allowing the "fiery darts"— that is, arrows with red-hot heads or wrapped with flaming tow** (see Psalm 120:4)—**to fasten and burn themselves out without harm.** It is compared to "faith" by Paul, but it is not the "faith in which we stand" (2Corinthians 1:24) or the "active faith" of Hebrews 11. The darts of temptation, whether from fear, lust, or doubt, fall harmless on the faith of patience and endurance, the almost passive faith, trusting in God's protection and subject to His will.

During my tribulation in 2013, I realized that my life was full of fiery darts that were coming at me quicker than I could endure. I had only just accepted that both of my breasts would have to be removed due to breast cancer suddenly my daughter became very ill, requiring an ambulance ride to the hospital. The doctor told me bluntly that my child's kidneys had failed, and that most of her organs would follow. These darts were coming at me so fast, you had to be kidding me.

I begin to descend into a deep, deep depression. Once I realize that no one in my entire life could solve it - but Jesus, I prayed to the Lord for guidance, and he provided me with a plan of escape, and I began writing down this plan and authored the book **"How to Trust God" (when everything goes wrong).** Using the tools He provided in this book, I was able to seek his guidance and realized that He was the only one who could help me.

I didn't want to let my husband and three other daughters down by giving up by allowing Cancer to claim my life. I knew I'd have to fight and embrace the **"ENTIRE ARMOR OF GOD."** Because I couldn't combat these darts with my own strength, I needed **"Beautiful Faith."** I surrendered to God, and he assisted me in developing a faith that saw me through the ordeal.

1 Peter 1:7 (NIV)

"These have come so that the proven genuineness of your faith—of greater worth than gold, which perishes even though refined by fire—may result in praise, glory and honor when Jesus Christ is revealed."

This scripture says, -.... *of greater worth than gold, which perishes even though refined by fire—may result in praise, glory and honor when Jesus Christ is revealed."*

God's will for His children is that we **rejoice always, pray without ceasing, and give thanks in all things** to Him, even during the unavoidable challenges of life that we all must confront - and in the midst of the varied hardships that all humanity must encounter.

Trials are a criterion that God allows to test and enhance our faith in Him, as well as to appraise and improve our trust in His Word - and we are told in the Scriptures to greatly rejoice in the Lord, even if we must suffer much pain and many hardships for a period of time.

One thing I realized in 2013 would be that God, knew me before I was conceived in my mother's womb, and as a result, he knew the trials and tribulations I would face on my way to achieving my purpose and promises. Take a glance at what the Lord said to Jeremiah the Prophet in the scripture below.

Jeremiah 1: 5 (NIV)

"Before I formed you in the womb I knew you, before you were born I set you apart; I appointed you as a prophet to the Nations.."

Long before we began walking on this earth, we were set apart, appointed by God. The difficulty arises when we lose sight of the one who selected us in the first place. The problems comes when we pursue the wrong things and end up with a huge void in our lives. The enemy notices the cracks in the door once this void is there. Don't get me wrong: you don't always have to cause or do something bad for the enemy to take your life hostage. Which is why it is critical to learn how to have **"Beautiful Faith,"** and otherwise unflinching faith in God's ability to **"FIX"** IT.

Lastly, **<u>"Beautiful Faith" is trusting the Lord with your whole heart</u>** and not allowing fear, doubt, people, situations or anything else to make you doubt Jesus' ability to **"FIX,"** IT.

We'll look at how to develop **"Beautiful Faith"** in the next chapters. Make sure you take good notes and write down your thoughts, as this will help you reflect on what you need.

Notes

Chapter 2
The Gift of Faith
(Saving Faith)

So, what does it mean to have saving faith? **Saving faith, is first and foremost faith "in Jesus Christ."** "Faith" in and of itself, no matter how sincere, is not sufficient.
We must understand where salvation, faith and the favor of God comes from.

To put it another way, saving faith is a free and undeserved gift from God, given solely to unworthy sinners, through which we personally acquire an indelible share in the whole salvation achieved for us by the Lord Jesus Christ.

When you comprehend that Jesus is the **source of EVERYTHING**, you'll know that having faith that Jesus saves, heals, satisfies all our needs, died and rose again for our sins and to make sure we have a heavenly home is crucial. When you understand that believing in Jesus and how God's ability to provide, you will understand how to start walking in Saving/Faith in Action.

Ephesians 2:8 (NIV)
"For it is by grace you have been saved, through faith—and this is not from yourselves, it is the gift of God—"

The **<u>Gift of Saving faith in Christ</u>** consists of three components:

(1) Knowledge
(2) Acceptance
(3) Trust

Read the following scripture and describe what you've discovered.

Hebrews 12:2 (NIV)
"fixing our eyes on Jesus, the pioneer and perfecter of faith. For the joy set before him he endured the cross, scorning its shame, and sat down at the right hand of the throne of God."

We can see how Jesus is the ultimate example. Christ faced adversity and persecution (Philippians 2:8-11), as well as temptation (Hebrews 4:15), yet He never wavered in His commitment to execute God's will (Hebrews 5:8). His willingness to persevere in the face of adversity stemmed from his belief that God could and would "work all things together for good" (Romans 8:28).

Jesus' obedience served to create the objective for which we should strive- the ultimate victory and recompense in God (Hebrews 11:13–16). Therefore, faith is such a vital gift - we must understand that Jesus paid the ultimate price so that we could have life more abundantly.

The Old Testament heroes who demonstrated faith, defined as a forward-looking confidence in God. Jesus is the ultimate example. God patiently awaited the final fulfillment of His promises so that we, the living, could have a chance to be saved. Christians should seek to live up to that privilege.

Read the following scripture and describe what you've discovered.

Galatians 2:16 (NIV)

"know that a person is not justified by the works of the law, but by faith in Jesus Christ. So we, too, have put our faith in Christ Jesus that we may be justified by faith in Christ and not by the works of the law, because by the works of the law no one will be justified."

John 5:24 (NKJV)

Most assuredly, I say to you, he who hears My word and believes in Him who sent Me has everlasting life, and shall not come into judgment, but has passed from death into life.

It's not unexpected that you need to know something about someone before you can trust them. That is common sense, but what does a Christian and non-Christians need to know about Christ?

Non-Christians must understand that Jesus Christ died in their place and resurrected from the dead. That he made a willing sacrifice and possesses the ability to save.

We must understand that Jesus Christ died in their place and resurrected from the dead. That he made a willing sacrifice and possesses the ability to save.

Acceptance of His person and work is the second ingredient of saving faith.

The words **believe and faith mean "to accept something as true" or "to be convinced of something"** in the New Testament's original language. Someone may comprehend something (for example, that Christ died for our sins) but refuse to accept it as truth. The term **"believe"** is used in the Bible to mean **"to trust."**

Hebrews 12:2 (NKJV)

"2 looking unto Jesus, the author and finisher of our faith, who for the joy that was set before Him endured the cross, despising the shame, and has sat down at the right hand of the throne of God."

What does the author and finisher of our faith mean?

In the New Testament, the Greek word translated **"perfecter"** in Hebrews 12:2 appears only once. It literally means **"finisher" or "completer,"** and it refers to bringing something to a conclusion. When we combine the two words, we can see that Jesus, as God, both produces and sustains our faith. **We understand that saving faith is a gift from God, not something we develop on our own (Ephesians 2:8-9), and that this gift comes from Christ, its creator.** He is also the keeper of our faith, which means that truly saving faith cannot be taken away, lost, or given away. Believers will find this to be a great source of comfort, especially during times of doubt and spiritual problems. Our faith was created by Christ, and He will keep an eye on us.

In my life, especially in 2013, I had to realize not only that I needed Jesus' help to stay alive, but I also had to believe that all of my studying God's word and small leaps of faith would now allow me to walk in BIG FAITH.

I couldn't always see the raft for a lifeline, but I knew Jesus was the only one who could save me. Because I had been training on having little faith, I was convinced and didn't hesitate to place my trust in Him.

John 6:44(NKJV)

"No one can come to Me unless the Father who sent Me draws him; and I will raise him up at the last day."

You are not born again unless you have repented of your sins and believed in Jesus as He is written in the Bible. That means you haven't applied the measure of faith to the purpose for which God given it to you. Jesus is the only one who can atone for sin. He is the only one who can lead us to the Father. God wants you to believe in His Son Jesus Christ and repent (change your mind). Have faith in Him! He adores you so much!

Romans 10:14 (NKJV)

How then shall they call on Him in whom they have not believed? And how shall they believe in Him of whom they have not heard? And how shall they hear without a preacher?

Ephesians 1:13 (NKJV)

In Him you also trusted, after you heard the word of truth, the gospel of your salvation.

We often develop our faith through listening to other people's faith stories and hearing the Word of God preached.

NOTES

Chapter 3
Faith Revealed

Faith revealed- is to trust God, or to rely on God, it is to make a practical commitment. (**The Greek word** pistis, which means **"faith," also means 'trust.'**) Faith as trust, seen as an action rather than as an emotional state of confidence.

Belief in Jesus Christ, the Lord

Faith in Jesus Christ entails placing entire trust in His unlimited strength, protection, knowledge, and love. It requires accepting His teachings. It requires trusting that, even if we don't comprehend everything, He does.

Did you know that God uses faith to give us grace (that cannot be earned)? The Lord saved us for enteral death through faith by giving us grace to get things right and in order. How amazing is it that the Lord loves us so much that He has decided to give us grace through faith that we are worthy of His love and covering.

Ephesians 2:8-9 (ESV)

For by grace you have been saved through faith. And this is not your own doing; it is the gift of God, not a result of works, so that no one may boast.

The relationship between our lack of compliance, God's grace, and our redemption is clearly explained. Those who are saved by Christ are undeserving of it. By faith, God decides to forgive only based on kindness and grace. Paul will reiterate his point that human effort has no bearing on salvation in this section. No Christian can boast about his or her "goodness," because we are saved solely by God's grace, not by our own good works.

Amazing how God has given us this grace via faith that shields us and allows us to grow and develop in His goodness.

Romans 5:1-5 (NKJV)

“1 Therefore, having been justified by faith, we
have peace with God through our Lord Jesus
Christ, 2 through whom also we have access by
faith into this grace in which we stand, and
rejoice in hope of the glory of God. 3 And not
only that, but we also glory in tribulations,
knowing that tribulation produces
perseverance; 4 and perseverance, character;
and character, hope. 5 Now hope does not
disappoint, because the love of God has been
poured out in our hearts by the Holy Spirit
who was given to us.”

Now let us pay close attention to how **“Beautiful Faith”** is developed.

Romans 10:17 (NIV)

“Consequently, faith comes from hearing the message, and the message is heard through the word about Christ.”

“Beautiful Faith” comes **from hearing, and hearing comes through Christ's word**" (Romans 10:17). This "word" comes from God, who "inspired" (literally "breathed out") it through the Holy Spirit's action. Read Jesus' promise to his apostles that they would be guided into "all truth" with care (John 16:13).

"Beautiful Faith" is often revealed as you continue leaning more on faith and not by sight. Leaning on your faith is necessary in order to survive day to day. If you really want to see your life changed, just take 10 minutes each day asking the Lord to reveal to you how to start leaning more on your faith and not feelings or sight.

2 Corinthians 5:7 (ESV)
"For we walk by faith, not by sight."

We couldn't expect things to go well for us if we didn't have faith, no matter what the scenario was. As a result, faith is as vital as the air we breathe. Faith nourishes the heart and spirit in the same way that oxygen nourishes the body.

"Beautiful Faith" - can restore your faith in your ability to progress to the next level in life. It is as vital as the oxygen we breathe in. This is because having complete faith in your life will often keep you away from stressful events and individuals.

I remember having to remind myself to just breathe, just breathe during my 2013 fight for my life. The stress of the test(s) I was undergoing kept pushing me into a panicked state of mind. I became able to breathe and relax once the Lord revealed to me that this would one day be a part of my purpose. The Lord showed me the importance of having **"Beautiful Faith,"** which is simple, pure, and submissive

Hebrews 11:6 (ESV)

"And without faith it is impossible to please him, for whoever would draw near to God must believe that he exists and that he rewards those who seek him. "Jesus replied, "Truly I tell you, if you"

True, godly faith is characterized as trusting God, relying on Him in the future, and obeying even when we don't understand everything.

Abraham, Moses, and David, among the Old Testament's prominent people, all lived according to this style of religion. In the end, this implies trusting God's intention to keep His promises from an eternal standpoint. **Given the difficulties they endured, the faith model given by those individuals should motivate Christians to have a more confident and meaningful "Beautiful Faith".**

Everyone was created in God's image and deserves to live life to the fullest, according to our Christian faith. Having **"Beautiful Faith"** can help you move into the fullness of what God has planned for you.

What does true trust mean?

"Trust" literally means "a bold, confident, secure security". "For it is by grace you have been saved, through faith—and this is not from yourself, it is a gift from God— 9 not by works, so that no one may boast" (Ephesians 2:8-9). As a result, because of the faith we have been given, we trust. **Trust implies that we believe in God's promises in all circumstances, even**

when the evidence appears to contradict them.

Allow the Lord to work on your heart and belief system as you lean in to trusting Him more.

Notes

Chapter 4
Three Levels of Faith

1. Passive Faith (AKA- Little Faith)

A passive faith is one that simply acts as a result of others' encouragement. A believer who has an active faith is reliant on God; a believer who has a passive faith is reliant on the faith and support of others.

Matthew 14:25-31 (NIV)
Shortly before dawn Jesus went out to them, walking on the lake. When the disciples saw him walking on the lake, they were terrified. "It's a ghost," they said, and cried out in fear. But Jesus immediately said to them: "Take courage! It is I. Don't be afraid." "Lord, if it's you," Peter replied, "tell me to come to you on the water." "Come," he said. Then Peter got down out of the boat, walked on the water and came toward Jesus. But when he saw the wind, he was

afraid and, beginning to sink, cried out, "Lord, save me!" Immediately Jesus reached out his hand and caught him. **"You of little faith," he said, "why did you doubt**?"

2. Faith and Action (AKA-Great Faith)

Knowing the truth isn't enough to save your faith! Faith in action is surrendering to God's promises and allowing it to alter doubt or unbelief! It's refusing to accept the reality (what you see) and then forgetting about it as you hold on to God's truth. It's also known as faith in action, which implies that you're working or doing something to demonstrate that you're living by faith.

Matthew 8:6-10 (NIV)

"Lord," he said, "my servant lies at home paralyzed, suffering terribly." Jesus said to him, "Shall I come and heal him?" The centurion replied, "Lord, I do not deserve to have you come under my roof.

But just say the word, and my servant will be healed. For I myself am a man under authority, with soldiers under me. I tell this one, 'Go,' and he goes; and that one, 'Come,' and he comes. I say to my servant, 'Do this,' and he does it." When Jesus heard this, he was amazed and said to those following him, "Truly I tell you, I have not found anyone in Israel with such great faith."

Observe his great faith; Jesus recognized that the centurion was confident in Jesus' ability to heal his servant. This most likely resulted from being a desperate leader who had compassion for his servant and realizing that Jesus was his only hope. The more self-conscious we are, the more confident we will be in Christ. Herein, the centurion claims him to be the Divine HEALER and Jesus recognized his great faith.

James 2:22-26 (NIV)

"You see that his faith and his actions were working together, and his faith was made

complete by what he did. 23 And the scripture was fulfilled that says, "Abraham believed God, and it was credited to him as righteousness," and he was called God's friend. 24 You see that a person is considered righteous by what they do and not by faith alone. 25 In the same way, was not even Rahab the prostitute considered righteous for what she did when she gave lodging to the spies and sent them off in a different direction? 26 As the body without the spirit is dead, so faith without deeds is dead."

James 2:14–26 argues that one's actions—their "works"—indicate the type of "faith" they have. A so-called "religion" that does not drive a person to conduct good actions is not a saving faith; it is a lifeless faith. It's foolish and senseless to hope, or "wish," that a poor person will get well if such belief leads to no action. Similarly, James maintains that agreeing conceptually on some facts regarding God is insufficient. If a person's faith in God does not lead them to behave in accordance with their beliefs, then it is not saving faith. **It's just a personal opinion**. James never implies that faith isn't required for salvation. He never claims that work is required. To attain or maintain salvation He is adamant, however, that true saving faith must be accompanied by evidence of good acts.

"Works" are good and loving actions that result from genuine (saving) trust in God. Favoritism for the wealthy over the poor reveals a lack of trust. This is, in reality, a sin. Following up on these concepts, James declares that "faith" that does not result in good acts is dead. This type of conviction is nothing more than intellectual agreement. James does not dispute that faith in God is required for salvation, nor does he argue that good actions are required. He instead argues that works are to faith what breathing is to the body: a sign of life. a "belief"

Saving Faith can make us feel discouraged because there is no evidence that this occurrence will happen in the future. As a result, we lose hope, despite the fact that we know the Lord has plans for us to follow.

Psalm 37:23-25 (NIV)

[23] The Lord makes firm the steps
of the one who delights in him;
[24] though he may stumble, he will not fall,
for the Lord upholds him with his hand.
[25] I was young and now I am old,
yet I have never seen the righteous
forsaken
or their children begging bread.

One thing to keep in mind regarding biblical faith is that it always leads to more faith in our God. "Though he falls, he shall not
the believer's faith may be tested and they may stumble. (Psalm 37:24)

God knows that even though trials will test a believer's faith in this life, that trust should not be shaken because it is based on faith in God's promises, such as the promise of eternal joy with the Lord and the promise of "an inheritance incorruptible, undefiled, and that never fades away, reserved in heaven for you." Peter (1 Peter 1:4)

Mark 11:23 (NIV)

"Truly I tell you, if anyone says to this mountain, 'Go, Throw yourself into the sea,' and does not doubt in their. heart but believes that what they say will happen, it will be done for them."

Hebrews 11:1 (NIV)

"Now faith is confidence in what we hope for and assurance about what we do not see."

Hebrews 11:3 (NIV)

"By faith we understand that the universe was formed at God's command, so that what is seen was not made out of what was visible."

Hebrews 11:4–16 recounts examples of Old Testament figures who shown confidence in God and were rewarded as a result. Abel, Noah, Abraham, and Sarah are all praised for their faith in God's promises. This section of the book of Hebrews, in particular, concentrates on those who heard from God, obeyed, and were blessed. While their deeds are significant, the overarching theme of these early references is obedience to God when the fulfillment of His promises appears to be a long way off.

3. No Doubt Faith – Active Faith (AKA-Perfect Faith)

Active/Perfect faith is defined as never ceasing to pray, believing, and showing faith through deeds, which means always being on the positive side of life, so that when difficulties arise, our thoughts, words, and deeds are automatically aligned with our faith. According to your faith, be it done unto you, Jesus said.

Whatever the situation, we must not focus on what we are going through or what we see, but rather have hope through our "Active Faith," which will motivate us to keep moving forward.

We must recognize that faith in action is known as Active/Perfect Faith. When you demonstrate active/perfect faith, you believe and work to demonstrate your faith. Which mean you are doing something about your belief and taking action.

Faith and Deeds

James 2:14-18 & 20-24 (NIV)

[14] *What good is it, my brothers and sisters,*
if someone claims to have faith but has no
deeds? Can such faith save
them? [15] *Suppose a brother or a sister is*
without clothes and daily food. [16] *If one of*
you says to them, "Go in peace; keep
warm and well fed," but does nothing
about their physical needs, what good is
it? [17] *In the same way, faith by itself, if it is*
not accompanied by action, is dead.
[18] *But someone will say, "You have faith; I*
have deeds." "Show me your faith without
deeds, and I will show you my faith by my
deeds."

[20] *You foolish person, do you want*
evidence that faith without deeds is

useless? [21] *Was not our father Abraham considered righteous for what he did when he offered his son Isaac on the altar?* [22] ***You see that his faith and his actions were working together, and his faith was made complete by what he did.*** [23] ***And the scripture was fulfilled that says, "Abraham believed God, and it was credited to him as righteousness," and he was called God's friend.*** [24] ***You see that a person is considered righteous by what they do and not by faith alone."***

During my life I have had ALL three stages of faith. I remember having **"Passive Faith"**, because I was living and believing what others say I could and should have. **A passive faith is one that simply acts as a result of others' encouragement.**

I also remember having **"Faith in Action,"** which was required to survive and flourish after divorcing my two older daughter's father and relocating to Georgia. I left with only a Toyota Camry full to the top and my two daughters. I realized things were not going to get any better, and if we were to survive, I would have to pick up my entire existence and move forward on faith. **It took trust in the outcome and action to move forward (Faith in deeds).** Never stop believing in yourself and demonstrating that belief through your actions.

Along with me, you will continue to grow in your faith. You will notice that your faith will expand during this third stage, which is defined by never ceasing to pray and believing (No Doubt Faith). This is the stage in which we should all strive to never stop praying and believing that God has you covered, and everything will work out for our good.

2 Corinthians 5:6-7 (NKJV)

6 Therefore, being always of good courage,
and knowing that while we are at home in the
body we are absent from the Lord
7 for we walk by faith, not by sight"

Matthew 21:18-21 (NKJV))

The Fig Tree Withered

"18 Now in the morning, as He returned to the
city, He was hungry. 19 And seeing a fig tree by
the road, He came to it and found nothing on it
but leaves, and said to it, "Let no fruit grow on
you ever again." Immediately the fig tree
withered away.

The Lesson of the Withered Fig Tree

20 And when the disciples saw it, they
marveled, saying "How did the fig tree wither
away so soon?"
21 So Jesus answered and said to them,
"Assuredly, I say to you, if you have faith and
do not doubt, you will not only do what was
done to the fig tree, but also if you say to this
mountain, 'Be removed and be cast into the
sea,' it will be done."

Matthew 17:20 (NIV)

"He replied, "Because you have so little faith. Truly I tell you, if you have faith as small as a mustard seed, you can say to

this mountain, 'Move from here to there,' and it will move. Nothing will be impossible for you."

<u>A perfect example of "No Doubt- Action Faith" would be the Woman with the issue of Blood.</u> She used *"Now faith is confidence in what we hope for and assurance about what we do not see."*

Mark 5:24-34 (New American Standard Bible-NASB)

*24 And He went off with him; and a large
crowd was following Him and pressing in on
Him 25 A woman who had had a hemorrhage
for twelve years, 26 and had endured much at
the hands of many physicians, and had spent
all that she had and was not helped at all, but
instead had become worse— 27 after hearing
about Jesus, she came up in the crowd behind
Him and touched His cloak. 28 For she had been
saying to herself, "If I just touch His garments,
I will get well." 29 And immediately the flow of
her blood was dried up; and she felt in her
body that she was healed of her disease. 30 And
immediately Jesus, perceiving in Himself that*

power from Him had gone out, turned around in the crowd and said, "Who touched My garments?" [31] *And His disciples said to Him, "You see the crowd pressing in on You, and You say, 'Who touched Me?'"* [32] *And He looked around to see the woman who had done this.* [33] *But the woman, fearing and trembling, aware of what had happened to her, came and fell down before Him and told Him the whole truth.* [34] *And He said to her, "Daughter, your faith has made you well; go in peace and be cured of your disease."*

Women who have had exceptionally heavy menstruation know that it may be both uncomfortable and disconcerting, even if it does not entail painful, "pouring" blood. In the case of this woman, her illness is likely to be serious enough to cause persistent anemia and significant discomfort.

During these Biblical times, Menstrual blood and unused sperm were seen as life lost, similar to death, in Judaism. The woman's bleeding causes her to be handled in a similar manner to the leper in Mark 1:40–42. She is ceremonially filthy all the time. Everything and everyone she comes into contact with is filthy. Even if she stops bleeding, she must wait seven days to be ritually clean again (Leviticus 15:19–23), which may never happen for this poor woman. Menstruating women were not permitted in the temple.

This woman has been dealing with this problem for the past twelve years). Instead of being the adored daughter of a recognized official, she is destitute (Mark 5:26) and, due to her illness, most likely a social outcast, even among her own family.

Some medical disorders are still regarded as more honorable than others. For example, a broken arm is less socially embarrassing than hemorrhoids. Similarly, women are instructed from a young age to conceal any signs of menstruation. Jesus demonstrates yet again that He is unconcerned with social conventions. He doesn't mind if it's an injury, a disease, a birth defect, or even anything that would make us ritually impure if we were still following the Mosaic Law. In reality, God will occasionally utilize the most heinous bodily conditions to draw us closer to Him and aid us in our spiritual maturation to us our faith.

Imagine her knowing she couldn't go out in public, but nevertheless pressing on to receive healing from the Lord. The Lord bestowed on her will far transcend any suffering or discomfort, she **USED** her **No Doubt Faith – Active Faith.** She could either stay in the house and die, or she could use her faith to touch the hem of Jesus' garment and be healed.

Mark 5:33-34 (NASB)

33 But the woman, fearing and trembling, aware of what had happened to her, came and fell down before Him and told Him the whole truth. 34 And He said to her, "Daughter, your faith has made you well; go in peace and be cured of your disease."

Did you notice how Jesus said in verse 34, "*And He said to her, "Daughter, your faith has made you well; go in peace and be cured of your disease." Her "Beautiful Faith" made her well.*

She employed "Now Faith" by trusting in the LORD with all her heart and leaning not on her own understanding. She acknowledges Him and understands that He shall guide her paths.

First and foremost, we must place our trust in the Lord, not in ourselves or our plans, and certainly not in the knowledge of the world. We put our trust in the Lord because He is the only one who can be trusted. As a result, *"Blessed is the man who relies in the Lord and looks to the Lord for hope." Jeremiah 17:7* is a prophecy from the prophet Jeremiah.

Finally, Mark 5:24–34 interrupts a scene in which Jesus heals the daughter of a synagogue leader. He feels strength spilling out of him before he can get past the mob. God heals a woman who has been bleeding for twelve years after touching His robe. This chapter demonstrates that God is in charge of some of our distractions; He will occasionally give us vital job in the middle of other responsibilities. It also demonstrates that we are not a bother to Him. He never fails to make time for us. Jesus enjoys seeing us employ **No Doubt Faith – Active Faith,** which allows Him to act on our behalf.

What's keeping you from having "No Doubt Faith - Active Faith" right now?

____

____

____

What situation do you currently require "No Doubt Faith - Active Faith"?

____

____

Notes

Chapter 5
How to Activate Your Faith

Activating your **"Beautiful Faith",** is when we regard something as **"impossible"** in our lives, we call it a faith line. That is when we must put our **faith in Him, rely on His word, study all of God's promises, and dwell on them until trust arises in our hearts.** Never, ever, ever, ever, ever, be steadfast in your disbelief, but always keep growing in faith.

How To Activate Your Faith

1. Pray to God for the strength to fully trust in Him
2. Studying God's Word can help you stay motivated
3. Surround yourself around people of faith.
4. Begin to believe in the possibility rather than the impossible.
5. Show faith in deeds – by walking in faith.

Mark 11:24 (ESV)

"Therefore, I tell you, whatever you ask in prayer, believe that you have received it, and it will be yours."

James 1:3 (AMP)

3 Be assured that the testing of your faith [through experience] produces endurance [leading to spiritual maturity, and inner peace].

Jesus asked Jairus to activate his faith, by just believing that his daughter shall be healed.

Read the following scripture and describe what you've discovered.

Luke 8:49-55 (NV)

49 While Jesus was still speaking, someone came from the house of Jairus, the synagogue leader. "Your daughter is dead," he said, "Don't bother the teacher anymore."

50 Hearing this, Jesus said to Jairus, "Don't
be afraid;
just believe, and she will be healed
51 When he arrived at the house of Jairus, he
did not let anyone go in with him except Peter,
John and James, and the child's father and
mother. 52 Meanwhile, all the people were
wailing and mourning for her. "Stop wailing,"
Jesus said. "She is not dead but asleep." 53 They
laughed at him, knowing that she was dead. 54
But he took her by the hand and said, "My
child, get up!" 55 Her spirit returned, and at
once she stood up. Then Jesus told them to
give her something to eat.

No, unwavering faith in God is founded on God's very nature.

According to the Bible, God is all-powerful. It also tells us that God is good, wise, and loving. When you combine God's omnipotence, goodness, wisdom, and love, you get a God worthy of trust, praise, and adoration.

Romans 10:17 (NIV)

"Consequently, faith comes from hearing the message, and the message is heard through the word about Christ."

The author instructs them to put all burdens and weights aside. Do you have any plans for the holiday season? It could be a financial, relational, or even physical weight. "Lay aside sin," the author continues, "which clings so close." Sin is defined as anything that interferes with your relationship with God. The enemy's primary goal is to keep you as far away from God as possible, knowing that this is where your true strength lies. Put anything that is weighing you down or preventing you from growing closer to Jesus aside.

Hebrews 12:2 (NIV)

"fixing our eyes on Jesus, the pioneer and perfecter of faith. For the joy set before him he endured the cross, scorning its shame, and sat down at the right hand of the throne of God."

How to Build Your Faith
(Faith can be increased) -
Healthy and Safe Ways to Live - Out Your Faith Each Day

- Hearing God's Word is the foundation of your faith. Hearing God's word—the gospel of Jesus Christ—provides the first indications of faith in Jesus Christ.
- Pray and Meditation first thing in the morning.
- Faith is born of repentance.
- Covenants are the source of faith.
- Faith Is a Strong Concept
- Go on walks frequent
  in nature and read Bible verses.
- Participate in Small Group Bible Study Sessions.
- Participate in volunteer opportunities.

This measure of faith, which is so precious and valuable, is discussed in 1 Peter 1. One thing is certain: your faith will be tried, but you will be able to conquer it because you trust in Jesus Christ and will persevere.

1 Peter 1:7-9 (NASB)

7 so that the proof of your faith, being more precious than gold which perishes though tested by fire, may be found to result in praise, glory, and honor at the revelation of Jesus Christ; 8 and though you have not seen Him, you love Him, and though you do not see Him now, but believe in Him, you greatly rejoice with joy inexpressible and full of glory, 9 obtaining as the outcome of your faith, the salvation of your souls.

Notes

Chapter 6
Standing on Faith

Look at the below way to stand on Faith –

Now that we know what **"Beautiful Faith"** is, we must learn how to "STAND" and protect our faith walk as we continue to grow in faith daily.

You must be persuaded that the Lord is your main source of hope, and that Jesus will work with your faith to bring it to fruition.

The enemy and our flesh are constantly attempting to lead us away from faith and into a never-ending state of doubt. I remember encouraging my husband when we first got married to stop claiming we couldn't afford anything (such as a vacation) and asking him to stop speaking poverty over our finances. I taught him to say, ***"we'll have to postpone our vacation for a few weeks while we work out***

our financing plans". Isn't that a lot more appealing than ***"we're poor"***? God opened so many opportunities for us to succeed once he learned this way of thinking.

I brought this up because we must not only stand firm on faith, but also keep an eye on what comes out of our hearts and mouths. Negative attitudes and actions are hugely damaging to your faith journey.

Romans 4:17-24 (NIV)

[17] As it is written: "I have made you a father of many nations." He is our father in the sight of God, in whom he believed—the God who gives life to the dead and calls into being things that were not. [18] Against all hope, Abraham in hope believed and so became the father of many nations, just as it had been said to him, "So shall your offspring be"] [19] Without weakening in his faith, he faced the fact that his body was as good as dead—since he was about a hundred years old—and that Sarah's womb was also dead. [20] Yet he

did not waver through unbelief
regarding the promise of God, but was
strengthened in his faith and gave glory
to God, [21] being fully persuaded that
God had power to do what he had
promised. [22] This is why "it was
credited to him as
righteousness." [23] The words "it was
credited to him" were written not for
him alone, [24] but also for us, to whom
God will credit righteousness—for us
who believe in him who raised Jesus
our Lord from the dead.

Proverbs 18:21(NASB)
"Death and life are in the [a]power of the tongue, And those who love it will eat its fruit."

At its core (the tongue), a Christian's Christ-centered chastisement in one or more areas of life must be held accountable. Accountability and a gracious and forgiving mindset, as well as bearing one another's burdens, go hand in hand (Romans 12:16, Colossians 3:13,

Galatians 6:2). A relationship with Jesus will help you learn to control your tongue.

The tongue is a **fire as well, a world of evil among the body's parts. It corrupts the entire person,** sets his entire existence on fire, and is set on fire by hell itself. But no one can control his tongue. It's a restless evil packed with lethal poison, that is why we need Jesus to help us control the words we speak.

Matthew 12:36 (NIV)

"But I tell you that everyone will have to give account on the day of judgment for every empty word they have spoken."

."

In this scripture Jesus talks about, speaking is the natural outpouring of our emotions and thoughts. The Pharisees bear terrible fruit like a diseased tree. They are compared to vipers, implying that they are associated with the Devil and wickedness. Jesus emphasizes that we are responsible for every word we utter, echoing His teaching on God's complete righteousness (Matthew 6:1, 5, 16).

God must be obeyed

Satan delights in sabotaging your faith. Read James 4:7 below: "Then submit yourselves to God." The devil will fly from you if you resist him. If you're having trouble with your faith, it's probably because you're trying to combat Satan without totally surrendering to God."

1 Corinthians 1:9 (AMP)

God is faithful [He is reliable, trustworthy and ever true to His promise—He can be depended on], and through Him you were called into fellowship with His Son, Jesus Christ our Lord.

Concentrate on God's Might

The Apostle Paul's unwavering faith in God was founded on his intimate knowledge of God's greatness. At one point, Paul was in such dire circumstances that he believed death was the only option. Paul's ministry would come to an end if he died.

Nonetheless, Paul wrote in 1 Corinthians 1:9, "Indeed, we felt as if we had been sentenced to death." But that was done to make us rely on God, who raises the dead, rather than ourselves."

Even if he died, Paul knew that God could raise him from the dead. Even the worst-case scenario couldn't stop God. Even the great enemy of death is no match for my all-powerful, all-loving, merciful, and gracious God.

As a result, you can have faith in God. You are free to cast my worries on him. Cast your cares at his feet. His grace is enough for you.

I have seen great things happen in my life because I learned that God is powerful, and learning to lean on, trust in, and believe in Him has changed my life.

James 4:7 (NIV)

"Therefore, submit to God. Resist the devil and he will flee from you."

What areas do you need to resist the enemy and your flesh right now?

Pray

Prayer is the most effective way for us to communicate with God. If you have faith, you will receive whatever you ask for in prayer, according to Matthew 21:22. This informs me that God expects us to use this strong method of communication, and the strength behind it is our faith, not our word.

Trust Him

In everything, we must put our trust in Him. It's commanded in Proverbs 3:5, but Jesus says it again here. Have faith in God, complete trust and confidence in Him. Worry, stress, anxiety, fear, and doubt should never crop up if we have faith in God. If we have faith in God, we have complete faith that He will provide all our needs. We not only trust Him to provide for us, but we are also confident that He will provide us with an abundant life!

Read the Scriptures

Being fully persuaded requires consistent, daily exposure to God's spoken Word. This leads to us declaring or confessing what we believe, which is an act of faith that demonstrates our belief.

We must know God's Word! We must set aside time to sit and read our Bibles. We require His Word on the inside, in our minds and hearts. Knowing God's Word goes hand in hand with faith and prayer. Read His promises and then have faith in God that they will be fulfilled. Pray for them to be over your life. We will find strength, hope, love, peace, and joy in God's Word. We will also find promises of provision as well as instructions on how to avoid sin and rebuke the devil. Through His instructions, we will gain wisdom, knowledge, and understanding in our lives.

Read Matthew 17:20 and then believe that faith has the power to move mountains. Read Philippians 4:19 and believe that God will provide for all of your needs. Read Malachi 3:10 and believe that if you put God first in your finances, He will bless you to overflowing. Read Ephesians 6:10-17 and know that you have The Amour of God, no matter what comes your way.

If we want to practice faith in our lives, we must follow God's instructions and commands. By doing so, we will greatly strengthen our faith.

Take Arms

When your faith is being tested. The devil will try to convince you that God is untrustworthy. That's why Ephesians 6:11 urges us to "put on the complete armor of God, so that you can stand firm against the devil's schemes." You will be a sitting duck for the enemy if you do not arm yourself daily with the belt of truth, the breastplate of righteousness, the shoes of peace, and the shield of faith. While you're standing on faith, learn to be grateful for what you have.

1 Samuel 12:24 (NASB)

Only fear the Lord and serve Him in truth with all your heart; for consider what great things He has done for you."

Examine yourself

Are you allowing your emotions to guide your religion, or are you attempting to satisfy men rather than God? It's likely that you're questioning God if your faith is waning. Instead, Follow God rather than your emotions. You may not 'feel' loved by God or progress in your understanding of God. When the rains come, though, you will be able to remain firm in your faith. Place your skepticism in its appropriate context. It would be ridiculous to expect us to be without doubt, but does this mean that the moment doubt enters our minds, we allow it free reign?

Faith is a journey that lasts a lifetime. "I've been praying, I've been fighting, I've been trusting," you might say. I'd want to congratulate you on your perseverance…keep pressing to, **"Beautiful Faith".**

Philippians 4:1 (NIV)

" Therefore, my brothers and sisters, you whom I love and long for, my joy and crown, stand firm in the Lord in this way, dear friends."

1 Corinthians 16:13 (NIV)

"Be on your guard; stand firm in the faith; be courageous; be strong."

When we humble ourselves before the Lord and set our minds to gain understanding, discernment, and heavenly wisdom, we remain firm in our faith.

Finally, consider the verses below, which show how God's people maintained their faith and proceeded down the road to see the unthinkable become possible. I can personally attest to the fact that if you believe, God will make it happen. He not only healed my body from cancer, but He also healed my little Melonie, who went to be with Him in heaven. So, trust me, have that mustard seed faith, and let the Lord grow it into a great mountain of faith.

Matthew 17:20 (NIV)

He replied, "Because you have so little faith. Truly I tell you, if you have faith as small as a mustard seed, you can say to this mountain, 'Move from here to there,' and it will move. Nothing will be impossible for you."

Purchase a jar of Mustard Seeds (pictured here) to always have on your person as a reminder of the level of faith required to see God move on your behalf.

Jesus narrates the Parable of the Mustard Seed in the Bible, which is about faith and

the Kingdom of God. "The kingdom of heaven is like a grain of mustard seed, which is the smallest of all seeds on earth," Jesus says ...It grows to be the largest of all garden plants when planted, with such enormous branches that birds can perch in its shade.

Proverbs 3:5 (NIV)

"Trust in the Lord with all your heart and lean not on your own understanding;"

Romans 4:18-24 (NIV)

"Against all hope, Abraham in hope believed and so became the father of many nations, just as it had been said to him, "So shall your offspring be." Without weakening in his faith, he faced the fact that his body was as good as dead—since he was about a hundred years old—and that Sarah's womb was also dead. Yet he did not waver through unbelief regarding the promise of God, but was strengthened in his faith and gave glory to God, being fully persuaded that God had power to do what he had promised. This is why

"it was credited to him as righteousness." The words "it was credited to him" were written not for him alone, but also for us, to whom God will credit righteousness—for us who believe in him who raised Jesus our Lord from the dead."

Hebrews 11:5, 7-8, 11, 13 (NIV)

5 *"By faith Enoch was taken from this life, so that he did not experience death: "He could not be found, because God had taken him away." For before he was taken, he was commended as one who pleased God.*

7 *By faith Noah, when warned about things not yet seen, in holy fear built an ark to save his family. By his faith he condemned the world and became heir of the righteousness that is in keeping with faith. By faith Abraham, when called to go to a place he would later receive as his inheritance, obeyed and went, even though he did not know where he was going.*

11 *And by faith even Sarah, who was past childbearing age, was enabled to bear*

children because she considered him faithful who had made the promise.

13 *All these people were still living by faith when they died. They did not receive the things promised; they only saw them and welcomed them from a distance, admitting that they were foreigners and strangers on earth." welcomed them from a distance, admitting that they were foreigners and strangers on earth."*

The Race of Faith

Hebrews 12:1-2 (NKJV)

"Therefore we also, since we are surrounded by so great a cloud of witnesses, let us lay aside every weight, and the sin which so easily ensnares us, and let us run with endurance the race that is set before us,
2 looking unto Jesus, the author and finisher of our faith, who for the joy that was set before Him endured the cross, despising the shame, and has sat down at the right hand of the throne of God."

Mark 11:23 (NASB)

Truly I say to you, whoever says to this mountain, 'Be taken up and thrown into the sea,' and does not doubt in his heart, but believes that what he says is going to happen, it will be granted to him.

The point is that mountains do not move. They are the ultimate stability symbol. As a result, when Jesus speaks of mountains being moved or, more dramatically, 'thrown into the sea' as a result of faithful prayer (Mark ll:23; Matthew 21:21). Later, when the disciples asked Jesus why they couldn't drive it out, he made the statement recorded in Mark 11:23. The statement is remarkable and should be taken at face value. It also gives hope that anything is possible when one acts in God's will, in the name of Jesus.

"Beautiful Faith," my dear friend, is simply surrendering ALL to Jesus and trusting that He, and only He, can make things happen for you and for your own good. Now, tell your problems, desires and concerns **how big your God is…**

What kind of things has God promised to do for you?

- To work in you constantly until you are fully conformed to the image of Jesus Christ (Philippians 1:6).
- To provide for all of your needs with his glorious abundance (Matthew 7:11).
- To bestow divine wisdom on you as you navigate the complexities of life (James 1:5).
- To bear good fruit within and through you (John 15:5).
- To answer your prayers in huge, unexpected, world-changing ways (James 5:16).
- To never abandon or abandon you (Hebrews 13:5).
- To go above and beyond what you can think, ask, or imagine (Ephesians 3:20)
- Any many, many more

BONUS

Why Do Some Faithful Prayers Go Unanswered?

We must understand that sometimes we ask for things, and they do not happen the way we want them to, but we must remember that God knows what He is doing. I prayed so hard and had strong faith for Melonie's healing, even having attended several healing conferences, but it never happened. But in 2013 when the Lord revealed to me that her healing would take place in heaven rather than on earth, I KNEW IT.... He responded to my prayers of faith in the appropriate manner. Melonie was living on this earth with Cerebral Palsy, relying on others to meet her every need, but God changed that. Melonie went to heaven in 2013 and received her new body without any pain or restrictions. So, keep the faith and ask God for help.

Remember to always seek God's will and guidance when exercising your faith.

"BEAUTIFUL FAITH" PRAYER

Dear Heavenly Father, I come before you to pray that you show me how to grow in ***"Beautiful Faith"*** *and learn to trust you more. My heart's desire is to follow your plans for my life and live a life that pleases you.*

Lord, I acknowledge that my decisions and intentions are not always in your best interests; therefore, I surrender my life to you, dear Jesus, and ask that you teach me everything I need to know and teach me to trust you more and more.

In Jesus' name, AMEN

Notes

My Faith Journey

Keep a tablet of all your prayers of faith and how the Lord has answered your prayers and faith.

You can purchase the workbook/journal to go along with studying this topic from www.amazon.com

www.ingramcontent.com/pod-product-compliance
Lightning Source LLC
La Vergne TN
LVHW010457160826
845677LV00012B/2533

* 9 7 9 8 8 1 1 5 7 9 3 5 8 *